21 And The Hole

Jenaye Roger

Presentation by *BookLeaf Publishing*

Web: www.bookleafpub.com

E-mail: info@bookleafpub.com

ISBN: 9789357697170

First edition 2023

ACKNOWLEDGEMENT

I have to start by thanking my awesome mom, Lana. From reading early drafts to giving me advice on the cover to keeping me focused so I could edit, she was as important to this book getting done as I was. Thank you so much, mom.

PREFACE

The idea for this book came to me through a person, my mom. She encouraged me to share my gift and how I view things. I often view things as black and white, there's the good, the bad, and The Outside and The Hole. Talking and writing about things can often get you out of a rut and that's what happened; I got out of my rut, The Hole and wrote this book. The Hole takes on many shapes and forms and each story will share its form.

Life is short and you can't spend it all in a hole.
That's not how the saying goes but you get my point.

The process of writing this book was long and hard but worth it in so many ways. At the time of writing this book, I was able to crawl out of The Hole and go for what I really wanted, Life at 21.

My First Poem

I feel so sad, I feel so blue, so I wrote this poem just for you.

I've been feeling sad, sad in the dump. I feel like a big blue-black clump.

I have lost the bright light that shows the way, and I do not want to live another day.

Sometimes I think of hurting myself so I can go above, but then I think of those that I love.

Grade 4

Age 9

What I Lost

I lost my father before I knew,
What not having him would put
me through.

There was a wave of dark and dim,
That swallowed him whole
vanishing him.

An entire ocean separates us two,
or perhaps it's the line I drew.

A score that swept and sloped
through the sea,
Separates us like cold corroded
calligraphy.

The phrase I wrote in the gap, was
different but true.
 Maybe I did need someone, maybe
I needed you.

I never saw how deep his words did cut.
Now I'm sat in a fatherless rut.

Now I have his number logged in my phone,
so tell me why I still feel so alone.

Age 17
Grade 11

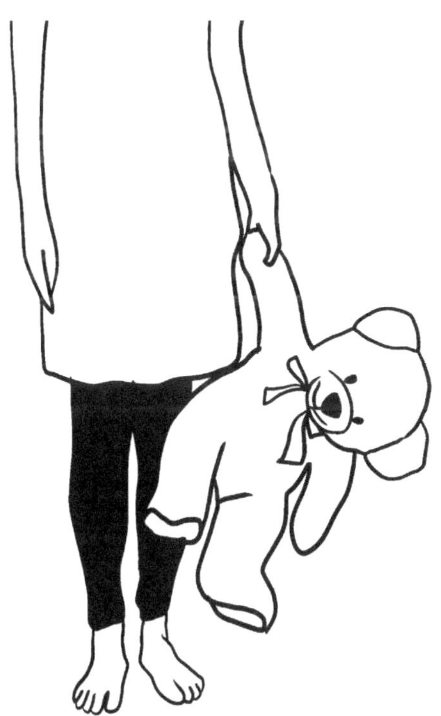

What I've Found

Compassionate and Gentle like a
mother dove,
you nurtured me from young with
all your love.

My mom is kind and warm like a
sunny day,
she has a smile that'll take your
blues away.

She loves you just as you are,
my mom is the brightest star.

Unique and Funny, always there to
rub my tummy.
She's grace and beauty all in one,
who could ask for a better one!

I love you mom, that is true.
Today, I dedicate this poem to you.

Age 21

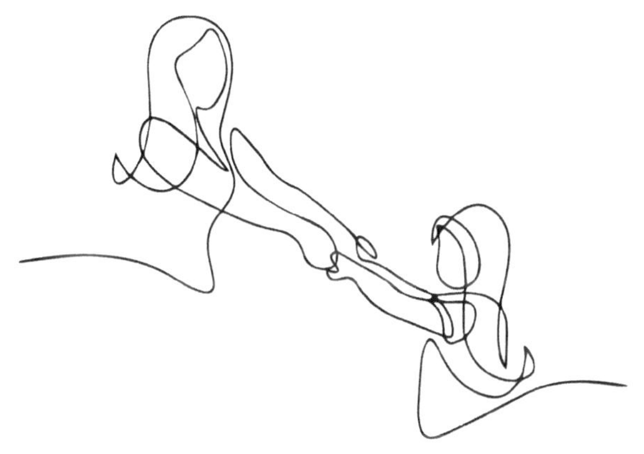

Deep Sorry Sorrow

Sorry is the word, that can't begin
to explain how I feel.
Disappointed is the word for you to
feel towards me

I cannot be trusted and feel hurt
and sad.
Most of the time I feel really, really
mad.

When the sky is filled with sun and
air,
all I can seem to feel is deep
despair.

While you all teach your students
with joy and pride,
I am the lonely one; cast to the side.

Ashamed Yes, Happy No, Sad Yes
and Stupid Yes So.

I wish I could make you feel proud
or happy of me, but that simply
isn't in my dictionary.

You're a wonderful teacher, who is
so fun.
I wonder if you've noticed, I'm the
sad one.

Sitting at the back hoping no one
sees.
I'm not happy, I'm truly sad you see.

When others are excited for what
comes ahead.
I live in fear, feeling like the dead.

I wish things were easier and more
understandable,
I wish I wasn't dumb and
noncompatible.

I feel so lost, so deranged.
I feel like people don't like me, they
think I'm strange.

I hope you see now, why sorry
doesn't begin to show how sorry I
am.

Have a great life and be joyful to the
end,
I hope you feel better and forget
this in the end.

Age 12
Grade 6

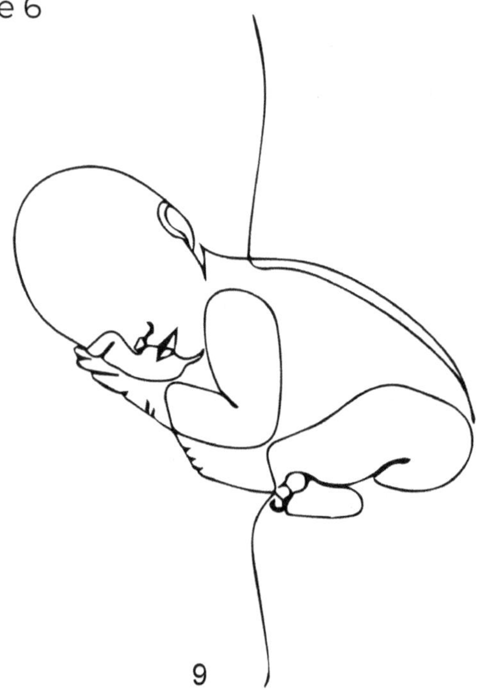

Sometimes

Sometimes you don't feel anything. You feel lost and confused like you've never had a use.

When you wake, you might still feel asleep and when you try to open your eyes, there's nothing. Nothing to grab and nothing to feel the joy of seeing.

Have you ever loved someone so dear you would crash into sadness if they ever let you go. To know they might not feel the same way, that'd you wish to never see the light of day.

To love something but to know you will lose them is something you can't bare. You start to feel sad, to feel blue and not care.

I feel out of place like people hate me, I feel like I'm something, not to be.

To be treated like you feel nothing inside, to be scrapped and pushed hard to the side. That you could never feel a punch or pinch; that you're not allowed to move an inch.

What do you say when someone says "shut up". Do you ignore or do you fight back. Having the feeling of fright just on your back, you wish you could say something, bite back.

I love my whole family, make no mistake. I have lots to regret and feel such hate.

Sometimes I feel alone, sometimes I don't feel anything.

Age 13
Grade 7

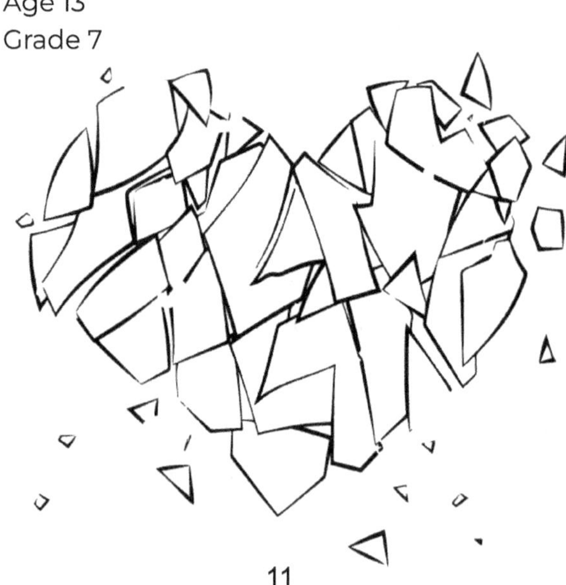

Why Is It?

It just isn't right,
the night too dark and the sun's too bright.

Crime is too common,
and love is forgotten.

Babies keep crying,
plants are still dying.

The world's too loud,
what's with this crowd?

Tears keep falling,
it's all so appalling.

Parents are too mad,
it's making kids sad.

I'm too tired to fight,
it just isn't right!

Age 17
Grade 11

Impact

You cover me in love and pain
and you remind me I'm the dragon,
and I'm to be slayed.

Words you say, make my day.
Kisses so true, left me unsure of
what to do.

But then you blew the whistle,
the situation hitting me, like a
missile.

He was the gasoline to my fire.
But everyone gets burned,
when you walk along the wire.

Desire took me out and Love pulled
me in.
It all just had me in a blur, tripping
in.

That was the danger before my
eyes,
Love is a mighty thing; especially in
disguise.

My first love was my first real
heartbreak.
Now I lie with this burning
heartache.

17/02/20

A Feeling

Knives like ice and eyes of white,
blinded by; love's bright light.

Unsure of what to do,
I continued to fall in love with you.

As if I knew it was a trap,
regardless; I fell in your lap.

Maybe I should've stopped.
But love is one strong temptress,
she sat and played with my mental
wellness.

A feeling, wonderful, deep and
bruised.
Something I didn't know; until I
met you.

17/02/20

Love

Love is gentle and kind.
Something quite often on my mind.

I think of him who makes me giggle
and of they who make me jump.
I think of those who get me out of, my
blue clump.

Love is powerful, it propels me forward.
Pushing me through the day
It's a big word, I love you; often scary to
say.

But it feels so great, to be loved by
someone.
That it feels no fun to be just you, just
one.

Love others, for you may not know,
that it's caused their fragile hearts.... to
grow.

Age 21

My Sleep

His sleep, is not deep
Like the snow pilling up on a steep

He gives his sleep a shake
And sobs until the tears make

The only other sound's the break
Of distant storms and birds awake

The sleep is bad, shallow and short
For the sleep is a beast with plans to
thwart

Until then he shall not sleep
He lies in bed with pillows that seep

He rises from his bitter bed
With thoughts of danger that he dreads

And though he fell, like an old oak tree
He did remember, what it was to be free

Age 17
Grade 11

Highschool

Highschool.

Apart from the flock is what I was.
They pulled me apart, using their
claws.

Away from everyone doing the same,
No one ever seemed to say my name.

Walking the halls with my headphones
on,
I never knew what was going on.

The whispers, the stares and the glares
all around.
I knew better than to make a sound.

People treating me normally was a
myth.
If only they knew I wasn't to be toyed
with.

Age 21

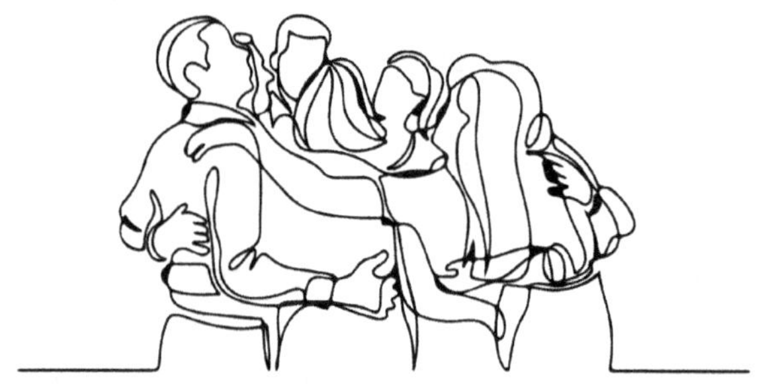

Black

The Shade that scares me,
and the colour everyone fears.

"It's too dark in here" and "He's
Black" seem to carry the same
connotation these days.

Fear. Those that are Black have
more to fear. You hear in court
"Black Lives Matter". Yet Red keeps
flying, splatter, splatter, splatter.

We're all supposed to be from the
same damn nation?
Then why do "He's black" and "It's
too dark in here" carry the same
connotation!

Black

The colour everyone wants to be,
yet no one wants to be.

They either see person or servant
I've come to learn.
But I've still got so much to earn.

To not be stared at when I walk
down the street.
To not feel someone following, on
the heels of my feet.

I want change and that's a fact.
Maybe one day it won't matter that
my skin is, Black.

11/27/19

Age 18

My Heart

Ode to my heart
How it protects me from the dark

The way I feel it beat
When I see a special treat

Loving all who love
Even those above

So why hate and discriminate when
there's better?
Like loving rainy weather

My heart protects me from harm's way
It's the only one who's really there at
the end of the day

Ode to my heart
We will never be

Age 17
Grade 11

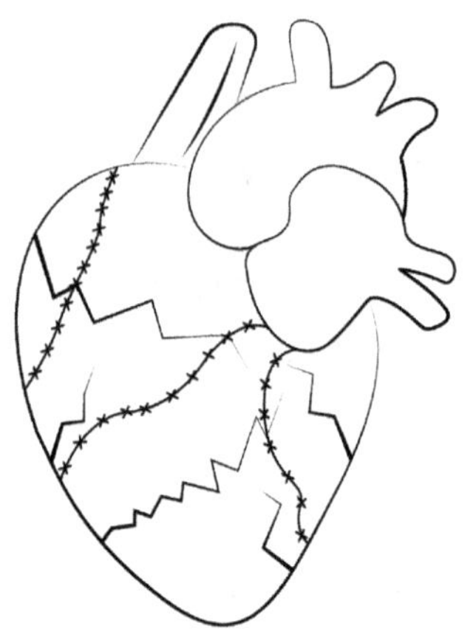

My Feelings for You

I loved you quickly
How else does one fall?

Your love brought me higher
Together we're tall

I love you so much
My hands start to shake

And I loved you so deeply
My earth starts to quake

I feel love in your chest
And its rise when you breathe

I feel it in your pulse
As it beats underneath

I love you so vastly
The ocean looks small

I loved you so quickly
How else does one fall?

Age 17
Grade 11

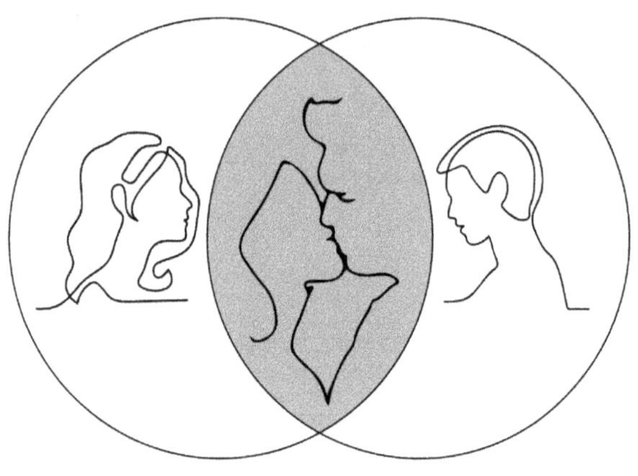

A Man

I trust too easily, because I wasn't taught
who to trust
They'd come in, trudge in and leave me in
the dust

They is a boy, who likes to play and who
likes to toy.

A boy isn't what I want but it's what I get
Immature and young, someone to regret.

I seek out those who are older, I assume
because of him
Yet they treat me like a child, I'm paper
thin

He regrets it, just like them all
He does stand weak, frail and not tall

I've come to grieve and come to learn
Now, it's finally my turn

07/10/20

Age 19

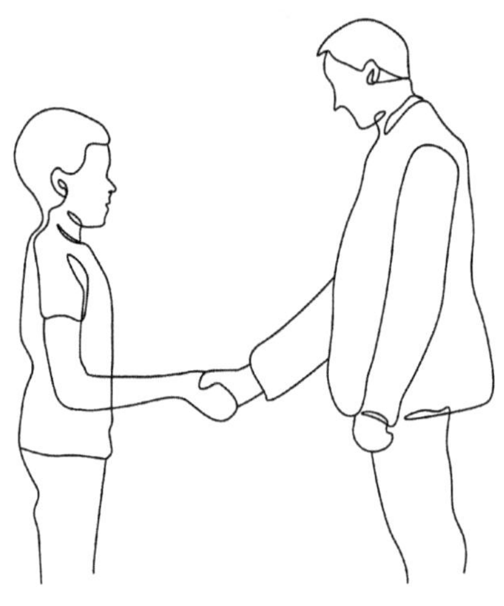

Lonely

Loneliness is loud
It's stranded on a cloud

It's lying awake with no escape
Loneliness is dark, with tight grips
on your heart

Loneliness is loud

I am the sole loner; in my hole,
where day is night and night is day
When I ask, everyday, why is it so
loud?

Loneliness is Loud

17/11/20

Age 19

The Hole

What do I write?
What do I say?

What happens when depression
comes to play?
When it's always night and the day
fades away.

The hole grows big and swallows me
whole.
I start to feel different, like I'm without
a soul.

It makes me small and weak, too afraid
to speak.

The Hole is a beast with teeth that cut
razor-sharp.
It picks you up and digs at your heart.

The Hole is my lion and I its tamer.
Its voice is loud it's a giant crater.

Age 21

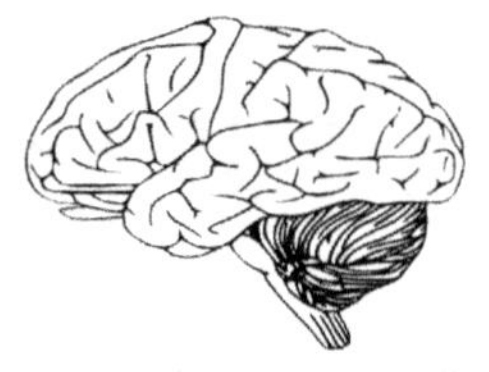

My Sister

I was once told, it gets better.

She told me this at one of my
lowest moments.
I felt horrible and sad like I was
missing components.

But the words brought me high
and made me strong.
For, the someone who told me this
is, is with whom I don't always get
along.

The someone who spoke words
simple but true, is my sister.
Someone I admire, her beauty is to
be desired.

She is older and wiser, and as tall as
a geyser.

Her glasses are made of glass and
she has endless sass.

My sister's advice saved me.
It gave me the will to push on and
live on

My sister once told me, it gets
better.

Age 21

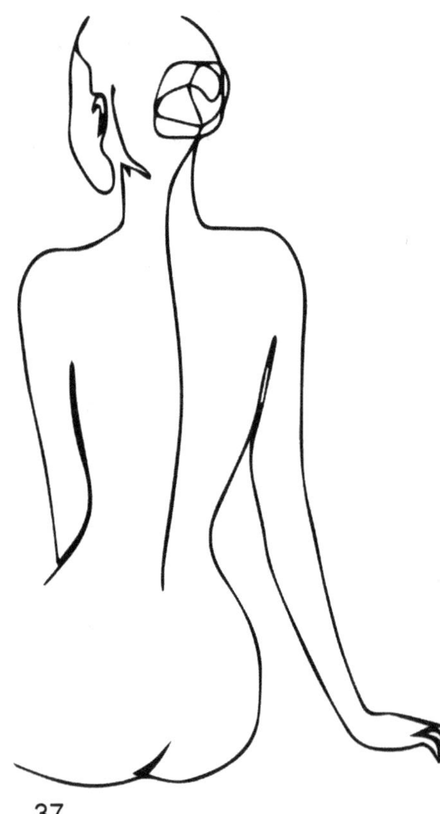

Spirituality

I believe in spirituality.
That there is something greater...
perhaps a creator.

Someone giving us strength when we
have none, sending us love when we
need someone.

I believe in spirituality.
That when you breathe in that warm
summer air, it's the freshness, of
mother nature's hair.

Her embrace feels like the soil between
your toes. Rich and thick. Taking away
all your woes.

I believe in spirituality.
That we can connect with those who
lie far beneath.
That they can touch us, deep
underneath.

Age 21

Daisy

My best friend of the time
is now asleep and lies.

Her pillow isn't next to me.
It's now in the clouds.

I can't hear her meows.
Yet the world still feels so loud.

I miss her soft fur and the way she'd
purr,
I miss her cries for love and I miss
her above.

Daisy was my heart and now we're
apart.
I miss daisy everyday, I know you're
with me, every step of the way.

Age 21

21

21 years, 261 months, 1110 weeks
and 7729 days have brought me here.
To this 21st poem in my 21st year.

I've learned to grow and take control.
To say what is mine, to find a goal.

I've taken hits, deep and true.
I've also learned it's better, to be you.

To be who you are and say what you
feel
It's all important, to truly heal.

This life is hard, this life is real
In this life I've learned to feel.

21 years, 261 months, 1110 weeks
and 7729 days have brought me here.
To this 21st poem in my 21st year.

Age 21

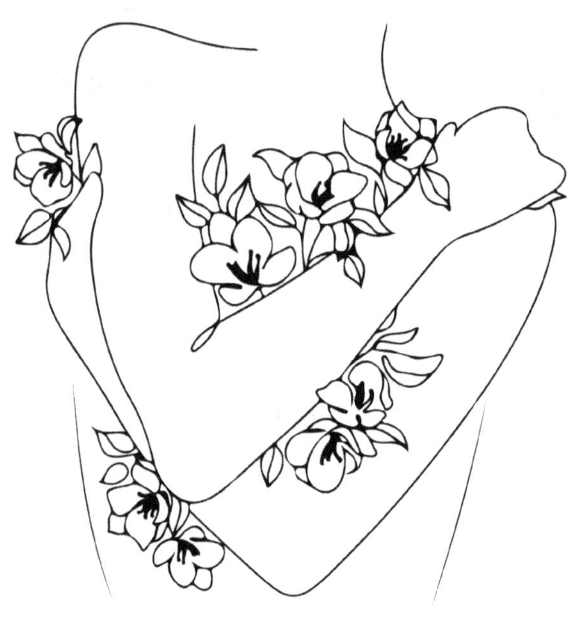